WILDCATS

Canada Lynx

by Erika L. Shores

Consulting Editor: Gail Saunders-Smith, PhD

Consultant: Robin Keith
Senior Research Coordinator
San Diego Zoo's Institute for Conservation Research

CAPSTONE PRESS
a capstone imprint

Pebble Plus is published by Capstone Press,
151 Good Counsel Drive, P.O. Box 669, Mankato, Minnesota 56002.
www.capstonepub.com

032010
005740CGF10

 Books published by Capstone Press are manufactured with paper
containing at least 10 percent post-consumer waste.

Library of Congress Cataloging-in-Publication Data
Shores, Erika L., 1976–
    Canada lynx / by Erika L. Shores.
    p. cm.—(Pebble plus. Wildcats)
    Includes bibliographical references and index.
    Summary: "Simple text and full-color photos explain the habitat, life cycle, range, and behavior of
Canada lynx"— Provided by publisher.
    ISBN 978-1-4296-4484-6 (library binding)
    1. Lynx—Juvenile literature. I. Title. II. Series.
QL737.C23S5455 2011
599.75'3—dc22
                                                  2010002796

Editorial Credits
Katy Kudela, editor; Bobbie Nuytten, designer; Svetlana Zhurkin, media researcher; Eric Manske, production specialist

Photo Credits
Alamy/Juniors Bildarchiv, 7; Spirit Wolf Photography/Nancy Greifenhagen, cover
Creatas, 15
Getty Images/Photolibrary/Bob Bennett, 17; Photolibrary/Daniel Cox, 18–19
iStockphoto/John Pitcher, 1
Minden Pictures/Matthias Breiter, 9
Peter Arnold/Wildlife, 21
Shutterstock/Dennis Donohue, 5; Fenton (paw prints), cover and throughout; FloridaStock, back cover, 11
Visuals Unlimited/Beth Davidow, 12–13

The author dedicates this book to her nephews, A.J. and Zachary Mikkelson.

Note to Parents and Teachers

The Wildcats series supports national science standards related to life science. This book
describes and illustrates Canada lynx. The images support early readers in understanding
the text. The repetition of words and phrases helps early readers learn new words. This book
also introduces early readers to subject-specific vocabulary words, which are defined in the
Glossary section. Early readers may need assistance to read some words and to use the Table of
Contents, Glossary, Read More, Internet Sites, and Index sections of the book.

Table of Contents

Forest Hunters

A Canada lynx creeps

through a snowy forest.

The wildcat's big paws step

lightly on the snow.

Canada lynx live in Canada
and the United States.
They make their dens
under fallen trees
or rocky ledges.

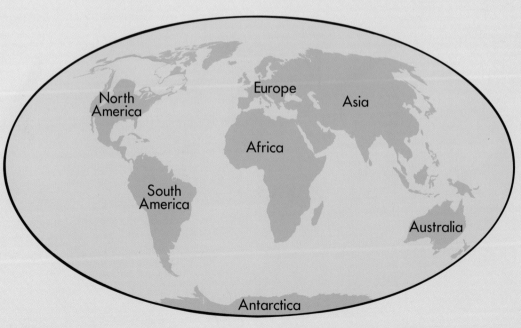

North
America

Europe

Asia

Africa

South
America

Australia

Antarctica

☐ where Canada lynx live

Canada Lynx Bodies

Canada lynx look like
big house cats.
They weigh up to
37 pounds (17 kilograms).

house cat

Canada lynx

Canada lynx have thick fur.
A ruff of hair grows
around their faces.
Tufts of long, black hair
grow on their ear tips.

Hunting Prey

The Canada lynx is
a sneaky hunter.
It hides and waits for prey.
Pounce! The hungry lynx
catches its meal.

Canada lynx mostly hunt
snowshoe hares.
When there are no hares,
these wildcats eat birds,
squirrels, and mice.

Canada Lynx Life Cycle

Adult Canada lynx

live alone.

In early spring,

males and females

come together to mate.

In May or June,

female lynx give birth

to up to four kits.

Mothers feed and keep

their kits safe.

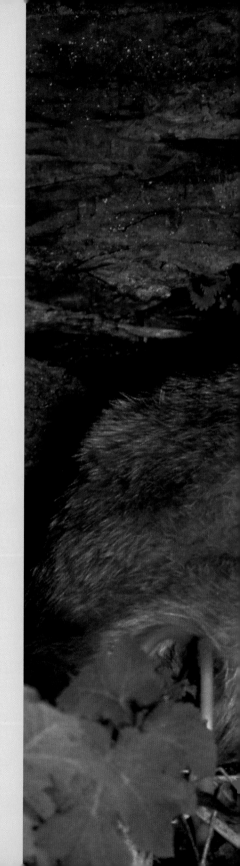

At around 10 months,

kits are ready to hunt.

They leave their mothers.

Canada lynx live up to

12 years in the wild.

Glossary

den—a place where a wild animal lives

kit—a young Canada lynx

ledge—a narrow, flat shelf on the side of a mountain or a cliff

mate—to join together to produce young

prey—an animal hunted by another animal for food

ruff—a ring of long fur around an animal's neck

snowshoe hare—a large-footed North American mammal; snowshoe hares are white in winter and brown in summer

tuft—a bunch of hair attached together at the base

Read More

Doudna, Kelly. *It's a Baby Lynx!* Baby Mammals. Edina, Minn.: Abdo, 2008.

Pitts, Zachary. *The Pebble First Guide to Wildcats.* Pebble First Guides. Mankato, Minn.: Capstone Press, 2009.

Internet Sites

FactHound offers a safe, fun way to find Internet sites related to this book. All of the sites on FactHound have been researched by our staff.

Here's all you do:

Visit *www.facthound.com*

FactHound will fetch the best sites for you!

Index

Word Count: 170
Grade: 1
Early-Intervention Level: 17